DIGGING FOR TREASURE

Expository Preaching: Proclaiming Grace and Truth

Edited by
David A. Hull and Paul Wilson

A  Publication

Published on behalf of MET by

MOORLEYS
Print & Publishing
tel: 0115 932 0643 web: www.moorleys.co.uk

ISBN 978 0 86071 702 7

© Copyright 2015 MET

British Library Cataloguing in Publication Data.
A catalogue record for this book is available from the British Library.

MOORLEYS
Print & Publishing
tel: 0115 932 0643 web: www.moorleys.co.uk

Contents

Methodist Evangelicals Together
is the largest independent organisation in British Methodism today, a renewal movement uniting and representing evangelicals at every level within our denomination.

Our three core purposes are:

- **ADVOCATING:** Promoting and representing evangelicalism within Methodism, and Wesleyan evangelicalism within the wider evangelical world.
- **EQUIPPING:** Providing resources through publications, conferences and our website for evangelicals within British Methodism.
- **SUPPORTING:** Offering pastoral support and advice to evangelicals, who can often feel isolated within Methodism and face particular pressures.

MET is a fellowship for every Methodist who shares our desire to:

- Uphold the authority of Scripture
- Seek Spiritual Renewal
- Pray for Revival
- Spread Scriptural holiness
- Emphasise the centrality of the Cross

MET promotes partnership in the Gospel to proclaim Jesus as Lord. Our partners include:

- Cliff College
- ECG
- Share Jesus International
- Inspire Network

Join MET and partner with us to:

- *Network with evangelical Methodists in prayer and action.*
- *Add your voice to 2000 others on key issues at all levels of the Methodist Church and beyond.*
- *Participate in national and local events.*
- *Receive the MET Connexion Magazine.*

Find us at: www.methodistevangelicals.org. uk

or write to us
c/o Moorleys Print & Publishing, 23 Park Road, Ilkeston, Derbys DE7 5DA
who will pass on your valued enquiry.

INTRODUCTION

David A. Hull
*Chair of Methodist Evangelicals Together
& Chaplain to Kingswood School, Bath*

It was a remarkable way for the apostle Paul to begin a letter: 'I always thank God for you because of his grace given you in Christ Jesus' (1 Corinthians 1:4). It was indeed traditional to begin a Greek letter with a prayer of thanksgiving, but we might be forgiven for thinking that Paul would struggle to find anything in the lives of the Christians in Corinth for which he could be thankful. Later in the letter, he would have some hard truths to share with them on a variety of subjects. Clearly, the Church in Corinth was in quite a mess, but the apostle Paul knew that grace and truth must always go together in authentic Christian ministry.

So, Paul began his letter with thanksgiving. What he chose to give thanks for is particularly striking: he thanked God 'because of his grace given you in Christ Jesus'. Paul thanked God for the Christians in Corinth because of God's work of grace in their lives. By its very nature, grace is given to those who don't deserve it. If it was deserved, by definition it wouldn't be grace. Paul was thankful for the Corinthian Christians because God had given them something they didn't deserve!

Surely, then, we can find a reason to be thankful for anyone because, as Charles Wesley wrote, 'his grace to all [does] freely move'[1]. As Wesleyan theology reminds

---

[1] Wesley, C., 'Father, whose everlasting love', *Singing the Faith*, no. 320.

1

us, God's grace is at work in the lives of us all, and has been at work even long before we could know anything of it. As we thank God for the work of his grace in the lives of others, we ought always to thank God also for his work of grace in our own lives, for we are as undeserving as anyone else.

Perhaps Paul's introduction to his letter reminds us that all our preaching, and all the other ways we seek to speak of God's truth, must be rooted in thankfulness. Thankfulness can bring transformation, in relationships, in ourselves and in the people for whom we are thankful. Let's be thankful for those to whom we have the privilege of preaching and, indeed, for all those with whom we are connected through the Church, even, perhaps especially, for those with whom we disagree or, for any reason, find difficult. God's grace is given to them just as much as it is given to us! If Paul could see that in his relationships with the Christians in Corinth, then surely we can see it in the Church today.

Paul adds that this grace was given in Christ Jesus. The focal point of God's grace and truth is, and always has been, Jesus Christ. The title 'Christ' reminds us that he is the promised Messiah, longed for throughout the pages of the Old Testament. We therefore cannot make distinctions in the character of God claiming, for example, that he was a God of truth in the Old Testament and a God of grace in the New. God always has been, and always will be, the God of truth and grace. Nor can we emphasise grace at the expense of truth, for they always belong together and can never be prioritised. As the years of waiting came to an end, John was able to write at the beginning of his Gospel, 'The Word became flesh and made his dwelling among us. We have seen his glory, the glory of the Only Begotten Son, who came from the Father, full of grace and truth' (John 1:14). As God's grace and truth came into focus in Jesus, God's glory was seen.

This publication considers how we ought to proclaim grace and truth together as we undertake expository preaching. The authors of the two key-note chapters in this publication, Chris Blake and Margaret Parker, both warn about the dangers of imposing a false dichotomy between grace and truth in Christian theology. The subjects have, however, been divided between them and they each consider the task of expository preaching from a different perspective.

Chris Blake considers questions concerning what constitutes 'truth' in contemporary, postmodern society. Appropriating the structure of David Bebbington's familiar 'quadrilateral' of evangelical emphases, he explores how preachers can faithfully and effectively proclaim God's truth when expounding his Word. This will involve a focus on the Bible, on the cross, on conversion, and on active discipleship. He challenges all preachers 'to read the scriptures carefully, to pray and to reflect deeply on those scriptures, and seek to understand, as best we can, the needs and experiences of those to whom we preach'. Above all, he encourages us to be open to and dependent upon the work of the Holy Spirit as we seek to understand God's truth in the Bible, preach that truth from the pulpit and apply that truth to the lives of our hearers, always striving to hold God's grace and God's truth together.

Margaret Parker explores the dangers of preaching truth without grace and of preaching grace without truth. She challenges preachers to make sure that we don't, on the one hand, 'make the gospel too easy by offering grace without the foundation of God's truth', and on the other, 'dispense so much paralysing guilt that our hearers [become] closed to the good news of the grace of God'. God's truth and grace ultimately meet in the cross of Jesus Christ. Margaret Parker therefore explores both the nature of the grace we are called to preach – which is both the character and the gift of God – and methods with which we can faithfully and fruitfully preach that grace, not only with our words, but also with our attitudes and with our body language. She echoes the challenge of another well-known Methodist preacher, the Revd Dr Donald English, who famously said, 'We don't need more arguments for the Christian faith; we need more free samples'.

An address given by Howard Mellor at the MET celebration during the Methodist Conference of 2015 is included as an additional chapter. A British Methodist Minister, serving as the Senior Minister of the Methodist International Church, Hong Kong, he traces the beginnings of Christianity in China and of Methodism in Hong Kong. He explores the factors which have led to the growth of the Church within a culture of repression and reflects upon some of the lessons British Christians can learn from the vigorous life of the Church in Hong Kong. The implications are very encouraging, insightful and challenging. The flow of God's truth and God's grace cannot be stemmed. The more it is pushed down, the more it overflows! The chapter concludes with a call to prayer.

I hope that the whole of this publication will move us to prayer. Let's pray for the spread of God's truth and grace throughout the world. Let's pray for those whose lives are especially difficult because they take a stand for God's truth and grace in oppressive cultures. Let's pray that God's grace and truth will come together in our preaching – and in everything we are, say and do – and that, in coming together, the glory of Jesus may be seen. It is fitting here to end here with a prayer penned by Charles Wesley:

> God of all power, and truth, and grace,
> which shall from age to age endure,
> whose word, when heaven and earth shall pass,
> remains and stands for ever sure.
>
> That I your mercy may proclaim,
> that all the world your truth may see,
> hallow your great and glorious name,
> and perfect holiness in me.[2]

---

[2] Wesley, C., 'God of all power, and truth, and grace', *Singing the Faith,* no. 498.

PROCLAIMING TRUTH THROUGH EXPOSITORY PREACHING

Chris Blake
Principal, Cliff College

'And the Word became flesh and lived among us, and we have seen his glory, the glory as of a father's only son, full of grace and truth' (John 1: 14).[3]

That verse, from the prologue to John's Gospel, is perhaps the most well-known example of the use of the terms 'grace' and 'truth' in the New Testament. It presents a wonderful vision of those two key aspects of Christian discipleship held together and embodied uniquely and perfectly in the person of Jesus himself.

St Paul, in 1 Corinthians 11:1, encourages his readers to 'Be imitators of me, as I am of Christ'. It's a challenging task in many ways, but perhaps particularly so in the task of holding grace and truth together, whether that be in our discipleship, in our witness, or, for those of us who are preachers, in the pulpit.

When Margaret Parker and I met to pray and plan the material in this publication, we agreed that the elements of grace and truth, which are held together in Jesus, should not (and perhaps could not) be artificially separated from each other. Jesus spoke truth with God's grace and offered grace within the context of God's truth. Our two chapters will therefore inevitably overlap

---

[3] Unless otherwise stated, all biblical quotations are taken from the New Revised Standard Version.

to some extent but, having stated that fact, I will seek to focus on truth in preaching, while Margaret will reflect on preaching with an emphasis on grace.

So, 'What is truth?' The question that Pilate asked Jesus is a good place to start. More specifically in our context here, the question is 'What is truth, and how should it be proclaimed in expository preaching in the twenty-first century?' I will mention in passing something about the 'How?' of the techniques of proclaiming truth through expository preaching, but that aspect of the subject is well covered in numerous books on the subject, and so I want to focus more on the questions of 'What?' and 'Why?'. To give some structure to the various thoughts that I will present, I will use what has become known as the 'Bebbington Quadrilateral' which seeks to provide an answer to the question 'What is an evangelical?'

David Bebbington is a historian, Professor of History at the University of Stirling, and a fellow of the Royal Historical Society. From a historical perspective, Bebbington identified four particular emphases of evangelicals. He described these as (1) *Biblicism* (the devotion to the Bible as God's Word); (2) *crucicentrism* (the centrality of the cross in evangelical teaching); (3) *conversionism* (the conviction that each person must turn from their sin, believe in the saving work of Christ and commit themselves to a life of discipleship and service); and, (4) *activism* (co-operating in the mission of God through evangelism and charitable works). This quadrilateral is, of course, debated and some would argue that although these four headings are helpful in understanding the development of evangelicalism throughout history, they are less helpful in terms of describing evangelicals today.

It is an interesting debate, but, in terms of this discussion, it may be that Bebbington's four headings provide a helpful structure for a conversation about proclaiming truth in expository preaching. I will use them to structure what I say, although, in order to relate the four headings particularly to the role of the preacher, I will use the following four headings: a focus on the Bible, a focus on the cross, a focus on conversion, and, a focus on active discipleship.

A Focus on the Bible

The commitment to an understanding of the Bible as God's Word is perhaps the key place to begin for a preacher. The Psalmist confidently proclaims, 'The sum of your word is truth; and every one of your righteous ordinances endures forever' (Psalm 119:160). It's an interesting verse that comes towards the end of the celebration of God's laws and statutes which is the theme of that significant psalm. Within the verse there is the important insight that God's truth is found not only in individual ordinances or laws, but also in what both the NIV and the NRSV describe as 'the sum of your word'. For the contemporary expository preacher, committed to preaching Biblical truth, this insight leads us in our preparation to consider not only the detail of individual verses (and indeed of individual phrases and words), but also to consider how such particular details sit within the wider context of 'the sum' of God's words to his people, as we reflect on the totality of the biblical record. If we are to be effective expository preachers who seek to proclaim God's truth, we need to study carefully our chosen text in order to understand fully the words and phrases it contains, but we also need to ensure that we step back so that we can see more clearly how that particular word or phrase or sentence sits within the wider context of the sum of God's Word as we consider the rest of the chapter, the rest of the book – and indeed the whole of the Biblical revelation.

The task of the careful exposition of God's truth, as contained in a passage of biblical material, has a long and honourable tradition within the context of Christian worship. In the second century AD, Justin Martyr (c. AD 100 to 165) described the place of what we might call expository preaching within weekly worship when he wrote:

> And on the day called Sunday, all who live in the cities or in the country gather together in one place, and the memoirs of the apostles or the writings of the prophets are read, as long as time permits; then, when the reader has ceased, the president verbally instructs, and exhorts to the imitation of these good things.[4]

For many centuries throughout history, the sermon was the key aspect of worship, and a letter written in 1692 and quoted in *The Oxford Handbook of The British Sermon 1689-1901* has (apart from its non-inclusive language) a somewhat up to date feel about it when it states:

---

[4] Justin Martyr, *Apology 1.67*

Many men have taken up the notion ... that the principal end of their going to church is to hear a sermon; that if there be no sermon, they have nothing to do there; or if the preacher be such as either they do not like, or cannot, as they fancie edify by, they may well be excused for staying away'.[5]

The contemporary context in which we are called to preach is, of course, very different from either the second or the seventeenth centuries, but, despite repeated predictions of its demise, the sermon, when prepared and delivered well, continues to be an effective way of conveying God's truth to God's people. The preacher is providing information, but, of course, the sermon seeks to do far more. David Day in his introduction to *A Reader on Preaching* notes,

> ... the recognition that scripture is not primarily a receptacle of information about God and the world. Scripture was written with the intention of effecting change. It does things as well as says things; it has a function as well as a focus. 'What is this text trying to do?' has become a critical question.[6]

So what does this mean for the evangelical preacher who has a high view of the Bible as the inspired Word of God? It means, I believe, that as we seek to proclaim the truth of the Bible, we need to use in an effective way all the

[5] Gibson, W. in Francis, K. A. and Gibson, W. (eds.) (2014) *The Oxford Handbook of the Modern British Sermon 1689-1901*. Oxford: OUP, p. 12.

[6] Day, D. *Six Feet above Contradiction?* in Day, D., Astley, J. and Francis, L. J. (eds.) (2005) *A Reader on Preaching: Making Connections*. Aldershot: Ashgate, p. 3.

resources available to us, as, in our times of prayer, study and reflection, we seek to understand the meaning of the passage on which we will preach. There are many textbooks available to help the preacher with what is called the hermeneutical task, as she or he seeks to convey God's Word in their own words so that it might again become God's Word in the hearts and minds of their hearers. David Day, in his helpful introductory book for new preachers entitled *A Preaching Workbook*, lists eight areas in which questions might be asked of the text. Expressed simply, those areas are as follows:

1. What is the literary form? Is it a letter, a poem, a song, is it history, prophecy or biography or perhaps a mixture of these things?

2. What is the context? What comes before or after, when did the event described take place, is this part of the letter an answer to a question that has been asked? What is the context within the wider setting of the Biblical book or the whole Biblical revelation?

3. What is the plot? In a narrative section, where does the passage fit within the developing story of God's people as told in the Old Testament – or in the ministry of Jesus or in the developing life of the early church as described in the New Testament? How does this particular part of the narrative reach its conclusion?

4. What is the text trying to do? Is it seeking to challenge or to encourage, to correct a problem or perhaps to call to faith?

5. What is the structure? In the verses being considered, do the words 'but', 'and', 'therefore' or 'however', or similar words, give some clue as to the flow of the argument?

6. Where are the points of contrast or tension? Does the passage include two ideas where one is included in order to emphasise a truth by showing its opposite?

7. What do my senses tell me about this passage? Do they describe something that I can imagine seeing, or feeling, or tasting, or touching, or hearing?

8. Where is the surprise? What is there in the verses being considered which challenges my thinking or the way in which I live?[7]

This is, of course, just one example of a series of questions that could be asked of a text. Each preacher will have their own way of getting into the meaning or relevance of the Biblical passage being considered. What is clear is that in order to proclaim the truth of a Bible text, we must begin by taking the Bible seriously as a resource which offers more than just information to the preacher and to those to whom they will preach. Preachers must begin by spending time with the Bible in allowing the Bible to speak to themselves first of all. The various exegetical questions that we might ask are important, but what is even more important is to allow the Bible to speak to us as we prepare. As Eugene

---

[7] Day, D. (1998) *A Preaching Workbook*. London: SPCK, p. 22-3.

Peterson has said, 'Exegesis is loving God enough to stop and listen carefully to what he says'.[8] There is something very important for the preacher in that statement. Reflecting on Peterson's words in his recent book, Jonathan Lamb, who has been involved in leadership roles in UCCF and in the Keswick movement writes,

> That's a great perspective on how to study scripture. Exegesis is seeking to understand the words, ideas and meaning of a passage and Peterson's point is that study is not the dull pursuit of technical jargon, but the way to encounter God and to hear his voice. Seen in this light, the work of understanding God's word is a demanding but a truly joyful and fulfilling task.[9]

So proclaiming God's truth through expository preaching begins by taking the Biblical material seriously - not simply as words which convey information but as words through which we can listen to God speak today.

A Focus on the Cross

The second of Bebbington's headings which he uses to describe evangelicals is that of 'crucicentrism' or a focus on the cross as the key moment in human history. Proclaiming truth through expository preaching will involve preachers having an appropriate focus on the death and resurrection of Jesus within their preaching. This does not mean that the preacher only has one sermon and that this is a sermon about the events of Good Friday. It means that true evangelical and

---

[8] Peterson, E. H. (2006) *Eat this book: a Conversation in the Art of Spiritual Reading*. London: Hodder & Stoughton, p. 55.
[9] Lamb, J. (2014) *Preaching Matters: Encountering the Living God*. Leicester: IVP, p. 62.

expository preaching cannot be separated from the message of the salvation that is possible as a result of the supreme act of love that we see in the death of Jesus. In 1 Corinthians 1:18, Paul reminds us that here is the key issue for those who would seek to understand the truth of the gospel, when he writes, '...the message of the cross is foolishness to those who are perishing, but to us who are being saved it is the power of God'. For those who don't understand its message, the cross is foolishness, but for those who do understand it, the cross is the central truth of the gospel. The task of the expository preacher is to guide people from a place where the cross seems foolishness to the place where the truth of the cross can change their lives.

So, how can that be done? The task begins by setting the cross within the wider picture of the whole of salvation history as we set our preaching within the wider context of the whole of the Biblical revelation. It has been said of the Baptist preacher Charles Haddon Spurgeon that, just as one might place a person in any village in England and they could find their way to London, so, in the same way, you could put Spurgeon down in any text in the Old or New Testaments and he would find his way to the cross. Some may argue that this is an unnatural preaching technique which fails to take the context of the starting text seriously. However, if we believe that the cross is not separate from, but is actually central to, the whole story of salvation history by which God has made his love known from the very beginning of time until its very end, then how can we preach without some reference to this central truth of the gospel message? The reference to the cross may be explicit or implicit, it may be the destination of the sermon, or it may be included at some point along the sermon's journey, but the message of the cross cannot, for the evangelical preacher who has an appropriate focus on the cross, be irrelevant to any sermon being preached.

We live, as has been frequently noted, in what is described as a 'postmodern' age. We live, therefore, in an age when many of the certainties and truth claims of the previous so called modern age are no longer seen to be relevant. We live in an age when many people no longer accept the idea of a 'meta narrative'; that is to say, they no longer accept the truth of a 'big story', a truth which holds all things together. For the preacher, and indeed for all Christians, this is a particular challenge for us in that, at its heart, Christianity is the ultimate 'big story', for it claims to make sense of all human experience from the initial moments of creation to those final moments when all will be gathered more fully into God's presence at the end of time. The message of the Bible, and of the Christian faith, is a message which holds all this together in a way which makes sense, and in a way which has its focus in the cross. Clearly not every sermon will expound the meaning of the cross in detail, but the interconnectedness of the Christian faith, in 'creation, cross and culmination', is at the heart of all that we proclaim.

So, what does this mean for the preacher seeking to preach God's truth as it is seen in the cross? It means that the preacher is called not only to preach about a Biblical text in depth, but also to preach about that text in such a way that their hearers can see how that particular passage of scripture finds a place within God's saving work which extends throughout all of time and which is most clearly seen in the cross. The message of the preacher is, therefore, to be focused on God and God's initiative in reaching out to men and women, in the wonder of creation, in the words of the prophets, in the witness of the church and in the self-giving love of Christ who through the cross and resurrection not only demonstrated love but also conquered evil through the power of God's love.

W. E. Sangster, in his classic book *The Craft of the Sermon*, retells the story about Bishop Stubbs of Oxford who, when his curate asked him what he should preach about, replied that the curate should '... preach about God and preach about twenty minutes'[10]. Interestingly, that story is often used in the context of a discussion about sermon length. It is perhaps just as appropriate in a discussion about sermon subject. As preachers, we should perhaps ask ourselves not only the question 'How long did I preach for?', but also the question 'Did I preach about God?'

Rosalind Brown in her book, *Can Words Express our Wonder?*, states that,

> Most people come to church hoping to draw closer to God. They are not looking for advice, instruction or command so much as invitation and encouragement to risk more faithful and creative living as baptised Christians.[11]

---

[10] Sangster, W. E. (1954) *The Craft of the Sermon*. London: Epworth, p. 172.
[11] Brown, R. (2009) *Can Words Express Our Wonder?: Preaching in the Church Today*. Norwich: Canterbury Press, p. 7.

If we believe that at the heart and focus of the Christian message of God's saving work is the message of the cross, then we can only preach that truth out of our own experience of living our own lives within a real relationship with God, and out of our own experience of coming to the cross ourselves. Calvin Miller, the Southern Baptist pastor who died in 2012, put this starkly and powerfully when he wrote, 'A good preacher brings to the pulpit good sermons from his or her private devotions. A great preacher brings to the pulpit great sermons from the presence of God'.[12] These are very challenging words all who seek to preach.

Rosalind Brown puts it equally starkly when she writes,

> We cannot preach unless we are prepared for God to be ever prising our life open. So, whether life is uncontainable joy, an aching struggle, or a pedestrian trudge, when we stand in the pulpit we bring not just our words but our life and we lay ourselves open to God and the congregation even if we say nothing confessional. Congregations can and will read us and our body language. They will see beyond our nerves or our confidence and pick up our approach to God's word, our faith, our concern for their well-being and our grasp of what is going on in their lives. They will know if we have dared to face their real issues and questions, bringing them to our prayerful engagement with scripture on their behalf, or if we have resorted to other people's generalities. They will also know if we dream of spiritual greatness for

---

[12] Miller, C. (2003) *The Sermon Maker: Tales of a Transformed Preacher*. Grand Rapids, MI: Zondervan, p. 121.

them, enlarging their vision and deepening their faith, or if we have no particular sense of where we are leading them. They will also listen for what we never say from the pulpit. All this will come across loud and clear whether or not we utter one word about ourselves.[13]

So the preacher seeking to preach truth will take the Bible seriously, and work carefully with its entire contents, but they will do so in such a way that speaks of the cross as the key moment in salvation history, speaking out of their own experience of, and relationship with, the holy and living God, and out of their own personal journey to the cross.

A Focus on Conversion
This is, perhaps, the aspect of Bebbington's definition of an evangelical that is most debated in terms of its relevance to the views of evangelicals today. In the past, the majority of evangelicals would, perhaps, have seen a particular moment of 'crisis conversion' as an important sign of a true believer. More recently, the understanding that, for many people, conversion is a process which takes place over a period of time has become more significant. What is clear, however, is that for the preacher seeking to proclaim the truth of the Gospel, the call to follow Christ (or to follow Christ more fully) cannot be ignored in their preaching.

There is a link, in the writing of Rowan Williams, the former Archbishop of Canterbury, between our

---

[13] Brown, R. (2009) *Can Words Express Our Wonder?: Preaching in the Church Today*. Norwich: Canterbury Press, p. 50.

consideration of the need for the preacher to nurture their living relationship with God and the offering of a call to faith. In words quoted by Rosalind Brown, Williams describes preaching as

> the telling of good news that makes a difference as the words of proclamation enact and enable change, witnessing to conversion in the preacher who preaches *from* conversion as well as *for* conversion.[14]

So preachers speak out of their own experience of the transforming power of God who has changed their lives, either in a moment or over a longer period of time, so that, in the image of 1 Corinthians noted previously, what had seemed foolishness is now revealed as the power of God.

Speaking personally as a preacher, I am always challenged by the end of Peter's sermon in Acts 2. On the day of Pentecost, empowered by the Holy Spirit, Peter preaches an expository sermon. He reflects on some passages from what we call the Old Testament, and he relates them to recent events in Jerusalem involving the death and resurrection of Jesus. It's a powerful sermon and one can imagine that Peter, filled with the power of the Holy Spirit, is preaching in a powerful way. It's not clear how Peter would have concluded the sermon because, by the time we get to v. 37, the crowd can wait no longer – they want to know how they can respond, and they cry out to Peter and the others, 'What should we do?' For the contemporary preacher it's a good question to write at the top of the notes we use when we prepare

---

[14] *ibid* p. 3.

to preach. We may have a sound exposition of scripture, and we may have related that exposition to the contemporary context, but have we answered the cry from the congregation, 'But what should we do?' In many services our reply will be about the challenge of discipleship, and we will come to that issue under our final heading, but surely, even with a familiar and traditional congregation, our reply will, on at least some occasions, need to include the invitation to 'repent and be baptised!'

Proclaiming truth for the evangelical preacher must, at the appropriate time, involve the invitation to faith, or to growth in faith, although in some contexts we may initially struggle to see why this is necessary. When I am preaching in the Chapel at Cliff College, for instance, should I assume that all there are so committed to Christ that the call to faith or to deeper faith is not needed? Many of us, I am sure, will be able to call to mind the names and faces of individuals who have, week by week, faithfully occupied their place in the pew (or perhaps have found their way to Bible College) for whom the personal experience of God's love and the personal response of a forgiven and accepted life remains a mystery. As with our focus on the cross, this does not mean that every sermon should have an explicit evangelistic theme or conclude with a call to kneel at the rail and make a first time commitment to Christ, but my own experience is that including something in the sermon or prayers which acknowledges that not all present will be certain of their place in God's love can be very significant for those present who might otherwise feel that the preacher's words are only addressed to those who have 'found' and have no relevance to those who 'seek'. Offering at the end of a sermon, for example, an opportunity for congregation members to respond to the challenge of the sermon can be important. At times I have invited congregation members to come forward during the hymn after the sermon and to stand or kneel at the front. At other times I have invited those present to take some symbolic action – such as tying a ribbon on a fishing net which has been draped across the communion rail. Such an invitation is offered in a gentle way and, unless an individual requests this, no one speaks to them or prays with them because this is business which is essentially between them and God. The response is often moving as people come to tie a ribbon as a sign of their hopes and prayers and as a response to what God has been doing, or what they hope he will begin to do, in their lives.

Preaching truth for the evangelical preacher will include taking the Bible seriously, it will involve a focus on the cross and it will include offering the call to conversion. We now turn to the fourth and final of Bebbington's headings, which, for the preacher seeking to preach truth, is perhaps the most challenging and potentially the most controversial.

A Focus on Active Discipleship
Clearly, as we have already stated, the task of the preacher is to do more than inform. We are not presenting a lecture, we are preaching a sermon. We are seeking to enable growth in faith and to make change possible in people's experience.

At the very start of her book on preaching in the church today, Rosalind Brown makes this point very powerfully in her reflection on the incident recorded in 2 Samuel 12:

> When Nathan went to see King David following his hushed-up affair with Bathsheba and the resulting death of her husband in battle, which had been carefully set up to look like an accident, he had an awkward message for the king. In effect, he had to preach a sermon that involved judgement to a congregation of one. How should he do it? We know from the story in 2 Samuel that he went about it in an extraordinarily effective way: he told a 'once upon a time' story about a rich man who killed a poor man's only lamb to feed a visitor. The effect was instantaneous: David was furious and pronounced judgement on the rich man, thus enabling Nathan to turn the tables and in four words to drive the judgement home: 'You are the man!' David immediately repented and Nathan announced God's response. In probably no more than three minutes, one of the most effective sermons ever preached was delivered: it had a purpose, knew its audience, had an appropriate methodology, unambiguous content and clear delivery, it engaged its hearer, evoked response and led to godly action.

'What more', writes Rosalind Brown, 'can we ask of preaching?'[15]

---

[15] *ibid* p. 1

Perhaps few of us are likely to face such a particular challenge to preach truth into such a sensitive moral or ethical issue involving royalty, but as preachers we need to address issues of truth which relate not only to the world of the Middle East two thousand or more years ago, but which also significantly reach into the lives of the individuals and congregations to whom we preach today. These issues might include, for instance, preaching on the truth that God heals to a congregation who have experienced the death of one of their number despite weeks and months of fervent prayer. These issues might include preaching on the truth of God's vision for human relationships and family life to a congregation where many present know the pain of broken and fractured relationships or where the commandment 'You shall not commit adultery' is not a subject that can be preached about in abstract terms. These issues might include preaching on the truth of God's call to unity to a divided congregation or, perhaps most challenging of all in our contemporary context, preaching on the truth as you understand it in terms of human sexuality, when the congregation present holds a range of views and will, in all probability, have a wide range of experiences of the subject within their family networks if not within their personal experience.

The examples that I have noted may be drawn from contemporary experience, but the challenge of preaching truth in such challenging contexts is not a new one. A familiar verse from Paul's second letter to Timothy begins with the affirmation that 'All scripture is inspired by God ...' but we must not forget that it continues '... and is useful for teaching, *for reproof, for correction and for training in righteousness*, so that everyone who belongs to God may be proficient, equipped for every good work' (2 Timothy 3:16-17, my emphasis). In case his readers miss the point, just a couple of verses later Paul continues, 'I solemnly urge you: proclaim the message; be persistent whether the time is favourable or unfavourable; convince, *rebuke* and encourage, with the utmost patience in teaching' (2 Timothy 4:1-2, my emphasis).

So what guidelines can we offer to the evangelical preacher who seeks to proclaim truth in the areas of personal and corporate ethics? Perhaps the following points provide some framework:

- Scripture does address issues of personal and corporate ethics and therefore these areas cannot be ignored by the preacher.

- Preaching about such subjects normally requires knowledge of the congregation so that the preacher's words are appropriately focused, although on occasions God will give the preacher a 'word of knowledge' to speak to a congregation that the preacher knows little about and the preacher should be open to that work of the Holy Spirit.

- In the words of Paul, offer 'rebuke *and encouragement*' so that the good is affirmed and the vision of God's Kingdom is presented alongside the challenge.

- Offer a framework which presents principles rather than a sermon which rebukes particular individuals. There is a place to challenge individuals about their behaviour, but it is not normally from the pulpit.

- On issues where the congregation is likely to be divided (perhaps on the debate between pacifism and those who support a 'just war', or in the area of human sexuality) the pulpit can be used to present an overview of the issues involved in the consideration of the subject. Such a sermon might serve as the introduction to a conversation planned for a later occasion when more than one voice can be heard and when different understandings of the subject can be honestly and openly shared in a context of confidentiality and trust.

This final guideline will seem to some to be about avoiding truth, rather than proclaiming truth. However, it is simply an acknowledgement that there are some issues on which Christians are deeply divided and on which those who describe themselves as evangelicals are found on both sides of the debate. Such contradictory convictions can be discussed in a safe and secure context in such a way that all present can grow in faith and understanding. Such a safe and secure context is unlikely to be found in a monologue sermon. It is at this point that truth and grace need to be held together with particular care.

So, in conclusion, proclaiming the truth through expository preaching will require the preacher to pay careful attention to scripture, to focus on the cross, to offer the call to conversion and to appropriately challenge the congregation to active discipleship. Proclaiming the truth is a task which cannot be ignored, but it is a task which must be undertaken with appropriate humility. Stephen Wright makes this argument well when he writes:

> No one person, no matter how gifted or authorised, has a monopoly on 'imaging' God through their speech. In fact, the image of the speaking God is reflected most fully not in preaching itself, but in the way Christians speak the truth to each other in love (Ephesians 4: 15). Given that our knowledge of the truth is as yet partial (1 Corinthians 13:12) and that we all still need to 'grow up' (Ephesians 4:15), this 'love' must include the humility to learn from the 'truth' that others have learned, and expose our 'truth' to their 'truth'. I take it that this is a key part of the picture of the organic growth of the body of Christ in Ephesians 4:16. Thus any claim to be speaking the 'word' or 'truth' of God, such as is made in preaching, must be made – if we are to be faithful to the humanness in which God has made us – not in presumptuousness, but in humility, prayer and hope.[16]

When Paul wrote to Titus, he indicated that the person appointed to be a church overseer should 'have a firm grasp of the word that is trustworthy in accordance with the teaching' so that they would 'be able both to preach with sound doctrine and to refute those who contradict

---

[16] Wright, S. (2010) *Alive to the Word: A Practical Theology of Preaching for the Whole Church*. London: Westminster John Knox Press, p. 123-4.

it' (Titus 1:9). To proclaim truth with grace, and to speak God's word with humility, is a great challenge and a great responsibility, but it is the work of the preacher.

A focus on scripture and the cross, and on the need to offer the invitation to conversion and the call to discipleship, are all important in this work. To fulfil this responsibility well, we need to read the scriptures carefully, to pray and to reflect deeply on those scriptures, and seek to understand, as best we can, the needs and experiences of those to whom we preach. Above all, as we prepare our sermons which speak God's truth, we need to prepare our lives as those in whom God's truth lives by the power of the Holy Spirit. David Heywood makes this point powerfully in his recent book entitled *Transforming Preaching*:

> Finally, the wisdom and power – by which the preacher discerns and conveys the word for the present moment and the community receives it and is changed by it – are those of the Holy Spirit. As preachers we need to welcome the work of God's Spirit in our lives and learn to discern the signs of the Spirit at work ... To be a preacher is to be open to the transforming effect of God's powerful word. This, perhaps above all, is the challenge of preaching.[17]

As preachers, then, we are called to proclaim truth, but we do so as followers of Jesus who was 'full of grace and

---

[17] Heywood, D. (2013) *Transforming Preaching: The Sermon as a Channel for God's Word*. London: SPCK, p. 30.

truth' and so we must strive to hold grace and truth together every time we preach.

This is the glorious message for the church that we read in Ephesians 4:14-16,

> We must no longer be children, tossed to and fro and blown about by every wind of doctrine, by people's trickery, by their craftiness in deceitful scheming. But speaking the truth in love, we must grow up in every way into him who is the head, into Christ, from whom the whole body, joined and knitted together by every ligament with which it is equipped, as each part is working properly, promotes the body's growth in building itself up in love.

PROCLAIMING GRACE THROUGH EXPOSITORY PREACHING

Margaret Parker
*Counsellor and former Vice-President of the Methodist
Conference*

Introduction: Balancing Grace and Truth

'The law was given through Moses; grace and truth came through Jesus Christ' (John 1:17).[18]

My focus is on proclaiming grace through expository preaching, but as Chris Blake has shown in his chapter, grace and truth belong together, with Jesus himself as the perfect and unique embodiment of both. Grace and truth are not opposites; the opposite of grace is law, and the opposite of truth is lies. Rather, grace and truth are like the twin wings of a bird or aeroplane, balancing each other, needing each other in order to function fully. As the historian Lord Acton wrote, 'Whenever you perceive a truth, look for a balancing truth.'[19] One without the other, we crash; both in place, we can fly.

To enlarge on this a little, we may say that grace without truth is weak, while truth without grace is harsh. Without the truth of the cross of Jesus Christ as the backdrop to our preaching, we are offering cheap grace, and not the true gospel. In this we do a disservice to our congregations, who need to know the cost of the forgiveness on offer. Not only that, if we preach easy

---

[18] Unless otherwise stated, all biblical quotations are taken from the New Revised Standard Version.
[19] Source unknown

grace, we are dishonouring God who gave his Son to die for us. At its extreme, the offer of easy grace leads to relativism and even immorality: 'certain intruders ... pervert the grace of God into licentiousness' (Jude 4). Perverted grace is a travesty of the gospel. In his book, *Vanishing Grace*, Philip Yancey quotes Shane Claiborne, 'I am convinced that if we lose kids to the culture of drugs and materialism, of violence and war ... it's because we make the gospel too easy, not because we make it too difficult'. [20] As preachers, let's not make the gospel too easy by offering grace without the foundation of God's truth.

On the other hand if we preach a message of condemnation, with no offer of grace and forgiveness, once more we dishonour God and we sell our congregations short. In my work as a counsellor, one of my clients was struggling in his relationship with God, with the church, and especially with the minister. He told me that he had said to his minister, 'If you can't offer me grace, don't offer me truth'. How right he was. Yancey echoes that sentiment when he writes, 'Often, it seems we are seen as more guilt dispensers than grace dispensers'. [21] How profoundly sad it would be if our preaching were to dispense so much paralysing guilt that the hearers' ears were closed to the good news of the grace of God. This is a recipe to drive our congregations to futile striving to become good enough for God; this is salvation by works which is a total contradiction of the gospel of grace. The message of salvation is good news, not bad news. In his paraphrase of the Bible, Eugene

---

[20] Yancey, P. (2015) *Vanishing Grace: What Ever Happened to the Good News?* London: Hodder & Stoughton
[21] *ibid*

Peterson graphically expresses John 3:17: 'God didn't go to all the trouble of sending his Son merely to point an accusing finger, telling the world how bad it was. He came to help, to put the world right again.'[22]

The theme of futile striving to please God is echoed in *The Prodigal*, the last book written by Brennan Manning.[23] Jack Chisholm, the fictional pastor of a huge church in Seattle regularly lambasted his congregation with the message, 'We must do better' – an unconscious echo of the powerless law given through Moses. Only when, through his own fault, he lost his church, his family and his self-respect did Jack Chisholm truly experience the grace of God, forgiveness and new life. The cross at the front of our churches proclaims simultaneously the truth of the consequences of sin and the grace of God in the offer of forgiveness through Christ. The good news we are called to preach is news of both grace and truth.

In this chapter, I would like to address two questions: 'What is the grace we are to preach' and 'How should we preach it'?

What is the grace we are to preach?
We are to preach the good news of the God of grace who saves us. The NIV Study Bible offers the following definition:

---

[22] Peterson, E. H. (2002) *The Message*. Colorado Springs, CO: Navpress Publishing Group.
[23] Manning, B. and Garrett, G. (2013) *The Prodigal*. Grand Rapids, MI: Zondervan.

God, grace and mercy of
The qualities of *God's character* by which he shows himself compassionate, accepting and generous to sinful human beings, shielding them from his wrath, forgiving them, and *bestowing* on them his righteousness so that they can live and grow in faith and obedience. Grace and mercy are particularly expressed through God's covenant with his chosen people and through Jesus Christ's atoning death on the cross.[24]

We see from this quotation that grace is both God's *character*, demonstrated by his compassionate attitude towards sinful people, and it is also his *gift* bestowed on us. The Greek word translated as grace is *charis*. *Charis* is both God's nature and God's gift of grace to us.

In his commentary on Ephesians, Warren Wiersbe writes about an evangelist friend of his who announced as his topic, 'Why Your Dog Does What Your Dog Does'.[25] Dog lovers came along because they were intrigued, but the answer was very obvious; he said, dogs do what they do because that is their nature! He went on to ask, why does a sinner do what a sinner does? His answer was: sinners do what sinners do because that is their nature. We can say equally, and with respect, that God does what God does because it is his nature. God's nature is grace, and he gives gifts to us springing from his character of grace. Our gracious God is supremely the holy God whose grace

---

[24] *NIV Study Bible* (1987) London: Hodder & Stoughton, thematic section 1055; my emphasis.
[25] Wiersbe, W. W. (1976) *Be Rich: Gaining the things that Money can't Buy : NT Commentary, Ephesians.* Colorado Springs, CO: Scripture Press.

is ultimately given so that we might be holy, as he is holy.

God's character of *charis* is unchangeable. His gift of *charis* is generous and immeasurable.

God's character of grace
Ephesians 2:4-8 overflows with the amazing grace of God, found in the words 'rich', 'immeasurable', 'mercy', 'love', 'kindness' and 'gift':

> But God, who is rich in mercy, out of the great love with which he loved us even when we were dead through our trespasses, made us alive together with Christ - by grace you have been saved – and raised us up with him in the heavenly places in Christ Jesus, so that in the ages to come he might show the immeasurable riches of his grace in kindness towards us in Christ Jesus. For by grace you have been saved, through faith, and this is not your own doing; it is the gift of God – not the result of works, so that no one may boast.

In these few verses we have a picture of the character of the God of grace who saves us, and the truth of our helplessness to save ourselves. The passage shows that: God overflows with love and mercy; we were spiritually dead to God; we could do nothing to help ourselves; God has taken the initiative and has made us alive in union with Christ; God has raised us up, and will continue to lavish his grace upon us. This is good news indeed; it is the heart of the gospel we are called to preach.

Of course, faith is required in order to access the grace of God, but even faith can be seen as a privilege graciously granted to us, 'for [God] has graciously granted you the privilege of not only believing in Christ ...' (Philippians 1:29). The *Expositor's Bible Commentary* says of this verse, 'Faith is not a quality, a virtue or a faculty. It is not something man [sic] can produce. It is simply a trustful response that is itself evoked by the Holy Spirit.'[26] When he tells the parable of the workers in the vineyard (Matthew 20), Jesus illustrates that we can do nothing to earn more of God's favour; the workers all received the same, however long they had been working.

St Paul's letters offer us majestic theological statements about grace. A Bible dictionary would send us on a treasure hunt revealing the amazing riches of God's grace. However, reading *stories* about God's dealings with his people will perhaps initially and more dramatically open the window to our understanding of God's grace. So as we read about God's gracious dealings with his chosen and often faithless people throughout the Old Testament, we can see clearly what grace looks like. We see God's grace in his patient dealings with Moses the murderer, with David the adulterer, with Elijah who ran away. And as we see the life of Jesus unfold through his interactions with those he met, his grace shines out; observe his conversation with the fallen woman at the well (John 4), with the woman caught in adultery (Luke 7), with the thief on the cross (Luke 23), with Mary Magdalene at the place of the resurrection (John 20), with two followers on the road to Emmaus (Luke 24),

---

[26] Kohlenberger, J. R. and Barker, K. L. (1978) *Expositor's Bible Commentary*. Grand Rapids, MI: Zondervan.

with Thomas who needed proof (John 20), with Peter by the lake after his three-fold denial of Jesus (John 21); these and so many other incidents show the supreme, generous, forgiving grace of God in Jesus. His compassionate healings, his calming of the storm, his feeding of the five-thousand all speak of his generous, graceful, loving character. No one reading the gospel accounts of his life and death could doubt that Jesus embodied grace in who he was, in what he said and in what he did, supremely on the cross where once and for all, grace and truth broke the power of sin and opened the way for us to know God. Grace is the character of God, Father, Son and Spirit.

God's gift of grace
Charis is not only the character of God, but also the gift of God to believers. It is the greeting which opens many New Testament letters, for example, 'Grace to you and peace from God our Father and the Lord Jesus Christ' (1 Corinthians 1:3). Grace speaks of the relationship between God and humans in Christ. The Applied Bible Dictionary states:

> The concept [of grace] uniquely expresses all that God has chosen to do for us in Christ, *the nature of the relationship God seeks with believers,* and the loving relationship God calls believers to establish with one another ...[27]

[27] Richards, L. O. (1990) *The Applied Bible Dictionary.* Eastbourne: Kingsway; my emphasis.

God does not sit in his high heaven, distant and aloof. He seeks relationship with us. That relationship is made possible by the death of Jesus who took on himself the sin which came between us and God. Andrew Moore graphically speaks of 'the abyss between God and humans which is spanned only by the arms of Jesus'.[28] Grace is not merely a theological concept to be grasped by our minds; God's gift of grace is something – Someone – to be accepted into our lives, a transforming power. God's *charis* is not a one-off gift, to be received once and set aside, like an unwanted Christmas present; it is an ongoing gift.

When I was thirteen years old, I became the Bible Reading secretary for a little Methodist church in South Leeds. This involved ordering and then distributing Bible reading notes to those who wanted them. It occurred to me that it may be a bit hypocritical not to read the Bible myself! So I persuaded my mum to buy notes for me, and for two years, every day, I read the Bible following the notes. By the time I was fifteen, I had met Jesus. I knew he loved me and I loved him. The grace of God in Jesus Christ found me, even when I was not looking for him. Grace is more than a great theological truth. It is the gift of the God who seeks the lost and who invites us into relationship with him. The gift is ongoing; we stand in it; we live in it; we can rely on it. Once we are in Christ we are, as we sing, a 'new creation, no more in condemnation, here in the grace of God I stand'[29]: 'Therefore since we are justified by faith, we have peace

[28] Moore, A. (2012) *Preaching - with Integrity*. Cambridge: Grove Books.
[29] Bilbrough, D. *I am a New Creation*. Eastbourne: Kingsway Thankyou Music 1983

with God through our Lord Jesus Christ, through whom we have obtained *access to this grace in which we stand'* (Romans 5:1-2; my emphasis). God graciously invites us into an eternal dance with him.

In the profoundly moving novel, *The Shack*, Mackenzie is invited, seemingly by God, to visit the shack where his five-year-old daughter had been brutally murdered.[30] Reluctantly, he goes and there he meets the God he blames for her death. If you read the book, you will discover that it offers an insightful, though very unusual, slant on the trinity. In the story the three persons of the godhead, who have a great time together, embraced into their lives the angry and hurting Mack. They welcomed him into their divine dance with open arms and open hearts, engaged with him, loved him and allowed him to find his way through his anger and grief, until he was able to *access the grace* of the godhead. Mack could say, with St Paul, 'We have peace with God through our Lord Jesus Christ, through whom we have obtained access to this grace in which we stand' (Romans 5:2). God the three Persons opens the circle to let us in. That is the amazing gift of grace we preach.

God's gift of grace in the lives of believers
We turn again to the words of the Applied Bible Dictionary:

---

[30] Young, W. P. (2007) *The Shack: Where Tragedy Confronts Eternity*. London: Hodder & Stoughton.

The concept [of grace] uniquely expresses all that God has chosen to do for us in Christ, the nature of the relationship God seeks with believers *and the loving relationship God calls believers to establish with one another*.[31]

God's grace flows into us and through us to other believers. So naturally, our churches are full of joy, harmony and unity! Is that a picture of your church? Well, maybe not yet! God does call us 'to establish this relationship with one another' but we are a work in progress, and though we are justified by grace through faith, we are not yet fully sanctified. God is relational, Father, Son and Spirit and, as with Mack in the story, God graciously calls us not only into relationship with all three persons of the trinity but also into a relationship of grace with each other. So in our preaching, in our leading of worship, we proclaim the grace, the *charis* of God, as seen in his character, in his gift to us and in our relationships with each other including in our relationship as preachers with our congregations.

A derivative of *charis* is *charisma*, meaning gift, plural *charismata*. *Charisma* is more specific than *charis* and is used in the various lists of the gifts of the Spirit, for instance in Romans 12:6-8 and 1 Corinthians 12:4. The *charismata* include the gifts of healing, prophecy, administration, etc. These gifts are given for a particular purpose, 'to equip the saints for the work of ministry, for building up the body of Christ' (Ephesians 4:12). The *charis* of God on the other hand is his eternal character

---

[31] Richards, L. O. (1990) *The Applied Bible Dictionary*. Eastbourne: Kingsway; my emphasis.

40

and the *charis* God bestows on us is his eternal pure gift which constantly pours from God to us.

G.R.A.C.E.

A popular, though perhaps somewhat oversimplified, way to define grace is: God's Riches At Christ's Expense:

God's ...
- God is the instigator of our salvation, when we were unable to help ourselves. 'God proves his love for us in that while we were still sinners Christ died for us' (Romans 5:8).
- It is because of who he is that God has chosen to save us. The Applied Bible Dictionary states, 'Grace ... uniquely expresses all that God has chosen to do for us in Christ'.[32]
- What is more, God acted even before we were aware of him. Theologians refer to this as *prevenient* grace, grace that *came before* we could do anything, for we were 'dead through our trespasses' (Ephesians 2:5) and therefore unable to reach out to God.

God's Riches ...
- The riches are God's to give as he chooses, for now and for eternity.
- God makes his riches available to us even though we do not deserve them and can never earn them. The riches are all gift. 'All who believe ... are now justified by his grace as a gift, through the redemption that is in Christ Jesus' (Romans 3:24).

---

[32] *ibid*

- God's riches are immeasurable, including 'forgiven-ness', new life in Christ, the power of the Spirit within us, the hope of glory and so much more. 'From [Christ's] fullness we have received, grace upon grace' *(John 1:16)*.

God's Riches At Christ's ...
- Christ's birth, life, death, resurrection, ascension and eventual return are key to what God has graciously done and continues to do for us.
- At his birth, Jesus became one of us, though he did not sin: 'For our sake [God] made [Christ] to be sin who knew no sin' (2 Corinthians 5:21).
- Throughout his life and supremely in his death, Jesus demonstrated God's love for us: 'I am the good shepherd. The good shepherd lays down his life for his sheep' (John 10:11).
- By his resurrection he defeated death for us: 'Where, O death is your sting? The sting of sin is death ... but thanks be to God, who gives us the victory through our Lord Jesus Christ' (1 Corinthians 15:55-56).
- Our salvation and our eternal future are totally dependent on what God has done for us in Christ.

God's Riches At Christ's Expense
- The cost of the riches bestowed on us was Christ's lonely, excruciating death. Misunderstood by the religious leaders, betrayed by a follower, denied by a friend, abandoned by all but the women and the beloved disciple, Christ went willingly and obediently to the cross, for us. Jesus said, 'I lay down my life for the sheep ... No one takes it from me, but I lay it down of my own accord' (John

10:18) and, 'the Son of Man came not to be served but to serve, and to give his life a ransom for many' (Matthew 20:28).

- Let us make no mistake; the cross of Jesus is not, as has been suggested by some, 'cosmic child abuse' perpetrated by God on his Son. The whole of the godhead chose the cross and felt the anguish of it. For 'God was in Christ, reconciling the world to himself' (2 Corinthians 5:19 REB). This was a plan from before the beginning of time; 'just as [God] chose us in Christ before the foundation of the world' (Ephesians 1:4).

We have seen how utterly amazing is the grace of God which is available to us and how glorious is the message we are called to preach!

How should we preach grace?

Other MET booklets offer guidelines on expository preaching. I focus here only on how we communicate grace by our words, intonation and body language, as well as by our attitude to our hearers. For, as Haddon Robinson states, 'When we address a congregation, three different communication networks operate at the same time: our words, our intonation and our gestures'.[33]

In *Transforming Preaching*, Jonny Baker explains that, when he asked people when they were last really inspired or challenged by a sermon, many of them pulled a face, and laughed, as if to say, 'Are you serious?' He writes, 'It is as though they cannot even imagine the possibility of

---

[33] Robinson, H. W. (1991) *Expository Preaching: Principles and Practice*. Leicester: IVP.

being inspired or hearing a brilliant sermon'.[34] As I read that, it occurred to me that it could be the lack of grace in the delivery of sermons which is the issue. Even St Paul could send people to sleep, as we see in Acts 20 where Eutychus fell out of the window as Paul was preaching. As we may not have Paul's particular gift of raising people from the dead, it's best not to risk boring our congregations. To engage our congregations we will use words which are understandable, sentences which are not too complex, voices which are modulated and gestures which match our words.

We have already noted that 'The concept [of grace] uniquely expresses ... the loving relationship God calls believers to establish with one another'.[35] That relationship between believers includes the relationship between preacher and congregation. Unlike listening to a sermon online, preaching with the congregation present is an encounter between people, as well as an encounter with God. As Jonathan Lamb has written, 'Preaching is a community event which requires the active participation of the congregation'.[36] As we model grace in the way we preach, we open the way for our hearers to engage with, participate in, and respond to what God has given us to say that day.

Grace should always permeate our preaching, not only in the substance of what we preach, but also in the way we

---

[34] Baker, J. (2009) *Transforming Preaching: Communicating God's Word in a Postmodern World*. Cambridge: Grove Books.
[35] Richards, L. O. (1990) *The Applied Bible Dictionary*. Eastbourne: Kingsway.
[36] Lamb, J. (2014) *Preaching Matters: Encountering the Living God*. Leicester: IVP.

preach it. Phillips Brooks famously stated that 'preaching is truth communicated through personality'. If our personality is lacking in grace, what truth are we communicating? The Revd Dr Donald English once said that we don't need more arguments for the Christian faith; we need more free samples. As our congregations watch and listen to us, we will communicate with them most effectively if they see in us the 'free sample' of the grace-filled personality shining through both what we say and how we say it.

Communicating grace by our attitude

RT Kendall has recently said, 'What will win the world will not come about by the keenest intellect humiliating an opponent, but by the most transparently Christ-like person melting hearts'. [37] It is a sign of grace to be humble, respectful, compassionate, non judgmental, patient, pastoral, and appropriately humorous, which all sounds remarkably like a description of the Jesus of the gospels.

Being humble

In *The Craft of Sermon Illustration* Dr Sangster has a helpful chapter on 'Mistakes Commonly Made'.[38] Number Five is, 'Don't glorify yourself'. He writes, 'All progress is progress in humility, and there are few spectacles more sad than that of a preacher unconsciously advertising in the pulpit his failure in this lovely grace'. We will have spent many hours preparing our sermon, but we are still,

---

[37] Kendall, R. T. (2015) 'Letter to the UK Church', *Premier Christianity Magazine*.
[38] Sangster, W. E. E. (1979) *The Craft of Sermon Illustration*. Basingstoke: Marshall Pickering.

along with our congregations, pilgrims on a journey. Arrogance will block communication.

In *View from the Pew* in the excellent magazine *Preach* the writer tells of his experience of being in the congregation: 'The preacher ... makes a joke about how lucky we all are to listen to him, and it doesn't sound quite sarcastic enough. Later he says we will struggle more with holiness than he does. It might just be me, but I prefer it when preachers put themselves down!'[39] Humility in us will help people to see past us, to God's grace and truth.

Showing respect
Grace is shown by the respect we show our congregations. Many will have more Christian experience than we do, will have read more books than we have, overcome more challenges in their Christian lives, led more people to Christ than we have. Their corporate experience should be acknowledged and honoured. We respect them by preparing carefully and prayerfully, by not talking down to them, nor using language which is too technical or showy. We respect them by dressing in a way that is neither provocative nor shabby, by making eye contact, and not preaching with our head in our notes. Knowing they are respected helps our congregations to engage with the message God has given us for them.

Showing compassion
Members of our congregations will be struggling with personal issues of which we are unaware. So if we are preaching, for instance, about greater commitment to

---

[39] Anonymous (Winter 2014) 'View from the Pew', *Preach*, LWPT.

the church in terms of time and money, let us be aware that some people struggle to feed their families or to attend worship because of shift patterns at work, caring for a relative, or supporting a wayward child. We offer God's grace, not misplaced guilt.

Being challenging but non-judgmental
I think it was Marge in *The Simpsons* who went on a church course about how to be more judgmental. Sometimes I question whether in the church today we need courses for that! Jesus challenged the unnamed woman at the well in John 4, but he did not use his knowledge to belittle or shame her; his challenge was clear but gentle. Finger-pointing and remonstrating are not likely to open many ears to what God is saying. Philip Yancey writes, 'When we are making condescending judgments ... the good news about God's grace goes unheard'.[40] Use of story or illustration will challenge more effectively than a direct attack, and if I use 'we' and 'us' when offering a challenge, I show that I am challenged too.

If there is a serious issue around in the church which calls for challenge, we may be well advised to let the Bible speak for itself. 'The word of God is living and active ... able to judge the thoughts and intentions of the heart' (Hebrews 4:12). Jonathan Lamb states, 'Our task is not to stand in front of the Bible text, but behind it, ensuring it is doing the talking'.[41] In a church newsletter, written when he was Vicar in Southam, Justin Welby explained,

---

[40] Yancey, P. (2015) *Vanishing Grace: What Ever Happened to the Good News?* London: Hodder & Stoughton
[41] Lamb, J. (2014) *Preaching Matters: Encountering the Living God.* Leicester: IVP.

'By all means do what you like, but if you ignore what God says is right you will be judged by him'.[42] David Hull says, 'The expository preacher simply exposes what is in the text, displaying the treasure for all to see'.[43] Sometimes that treasure will be a timely challenge.

In a church where the level of giving does not measure up to the lifestyles of the members, then offering examples of generosity will be more effective than rebuke, in the way that St Paul wrote to the Corinthians about the generosity of the Macedonians in 2 Corinthians 8. Or if there is known to be sexual immorality in the church, a positive message about our bodies being the temple of the Holy Spirit (1 Corinthians 12:15, 19, 20) is a gracious way of offering a challenge, particularly if the passage comes up in the lectionary or in a preaching series. The fable of the contest between the wind and the sun to make a man take off his coat illustrates the point that encouragement works better than hitting hard. However, if a particular person is behaving in an openly non-Christian way, a quiet word from a respected person will be a wiser approach.

Being patient
Acceptance of where people are in their journey towards sanctification will make our preaching more gracious and therefore more likely to be received. Paul instructs Timothy to preach and correct, with great patience and careful instruction (2 Timothy 4:2). You may be passionate, for instance, as I am, about house-groups, but when we preach about the value of meeting together

---

[42] Andrew Atherstone, The Road to Canterbury, DLT 2013, Southam Parish newsletter
[43] *Methodist Recorder,* 17 April 2015

in small groups, we cannot expect everyone to rush to sign up immediately. It can take a long time for some people to pluck up the courage to face close encounters with others.

Being pastoral
Particularly if we have a pastoral role in the church, we will have confidential information about people's struggles and failures. In our preaching we need to take care not to give the impression inadvertently that we are using that knowledge to challenge or shame individuals.

The *True Freedom Trust* (TfT) stands for celibacy for people with same sex attraction, but the leaders of TfT do not leave it at that. In a newsletter they explain, 'By concrete actions we need to be part of the solution caused by the problems of our dogma. Preaching a sermon ... and then sending them home alone is not enough'.[44] When we have a message which will be difficult for some people to hear, we should try to ensure that appropriate support is offered.

Using humour
Humour is particularly helpful when it illustrates a major point. Humour can bypass people's prejudices, and provide a handle to enable hearers to remember what they have heard. Humour should never be used at anyone else's expense, though we may appropriately tell a story against ourselves.

---

[44] *Newsletter* (Christmas 2014), True Freedom Trust, www.truefreedomtrust.co.uk

Using body language
In a helpful article in *Preach* the writer/preacher says,
'The service ... seems to be going well. But at the end
you wonder why people are trying to sidle past you
without shaking your hand. The truth is, while your words
conveyed grace and compassion, your body was shouting
judgment. You looked angry.'[45] Non-verbal messages
speak more loudly and more clearly than our words.

Conclusion
In this chapter, we have seen that grace is the nature of
God, it is God's gift to believers, and it is to characterise
our relationships with each other. St Paul wrote, 'I do not
count my life of any value to myself if only I may finish
my course and the ministry I received from the Lord
Jesus, to testify to the good news of God's grace' (Acts
20:24). We, too, are privileged to be called to testify to
the good news of God's grace. I pray that we will preach
truth with grace, and grace with truth and, most of all, I
pray that our preaching will enable our hearers to meet
for themselves the God of grace and truth and respond to
him, for the building up of his kingdom, for his glory.

---

[45] Swinney, J. (Winter 2014) 'Stand and Deliver: Skills for Effective
Communication – Body Language', *Preach*, LWPT.

VIBRANT CHURCH - EFFECTIVE MINISTRY: REFLECTIONS FROM THE EAST

G. Howard Mellor
Senior Minister,
Methodist International Church, Hong Kong

Howard and Rosie Mellor have served the Methodist International Church, Hong Kong since 2011. During that time they have visited China four times to meet government and church officials. In this article, based on the address given at the MET Celebration in the tent at Mornington Road, Southport at the 2015 Methodist Conference, Howard reflects on the ways in which the British Church could learn from the Church in China and Hong Kong.

It was an enormous privilege to address the MET Conference Celebration this year on the hallowed ground of the Holiness tent to which I first came as a student 'On Trek' from Cliff College in July 1968. The purpose of this chapter is to turn the spoken word into the written word. The following is my offering.

It has been a delight to serve the Methodist International Church, Hong Kong (MIC) over the last four years. It is a church of about 1,200 members meeting in eight congregations using four languages (English, Putonghua and two Filipino languages, Tagalog and Ilocano). I preach to them all in Yorkshire! Presently we are without a building, but more of that later.

It is an obvious point, but one often overlooked by British Christians, that the Church is global, missional, growing and its centre of gravity has moved from the West and North to the South and East. Ecclesial institutions are slowly catching up with this missional and structural truth. The arrival of Christianity to the steppes and coasts of China is a fascinating story.

Christian beginnings in China

Christianity came early to China. At a time when the Celtic missionaries Columba and Aidan were moving south from Iona and Lindisfarne, Nestorian Christians, most notably the monk Alopen (AD 635), were travelling east along the Silk Route into the western provinces of China where the church flourished for two centuries. The fall of the Tang dynasty in AD 907 completely wiped out the Christian community. The Mongul Yuan Dynasty, otherwise quite brutal, allowed a Franciscan mission and the resurgence of the Nestorian Church in the late thirteenth and early fourteenth centuries but during the xenophobic Ming dynasty Christians were repatriated or brutally murdered. However the most effective early mission to Chinese culture in the modern era was undertaken by the Jesuits in the sixteenth century, moving from their base in Macau up the Pearl River to Zhaoqing, an important administrative centre of

Guangdong. The most famous missionary was Matteo Ricci who wrote a treatise explaining the Christian faith using Chinese cultural images, *True Meaning of the King of Heaven*. The British came in 1841 claiming Hong Kong as part of the empire and a weakened China could not resist.

Today the church in China is flourishing. That is what almost seventy years of Communist rule and oppression does! No denominations are allowed, with all registered churches coming under the Three Self Patriotic Movement (self-governance, self-support, self-propagation), though there is a vigorous unregistered Christian movement. Three Self churches number over fifty-seven thousand. The policy is that they 'respectively reject' foreigners' influence on the church leadership, foreign financing and foreign missionaries. 'Patriotic' indicates the church's loyalty to China.

The pastors and leaders of the TSPM report to the State Administration for Religious Affairs (SARA), which is controlled by the Chinese Communist Party. The SARA is run by Provincial Officials and the relationship between the churches' authentic mission and the Communist Party varies from place to place. In some provinces the number of active (known) Christians is ten percent of the population and increasing, and the active membership of the Communist Party is ten percent and declining. Officials are worried about the rising influence of the Christian Church and its leaders. The National Security Law passed on 1 July 2015 by the National People's Congress Standing Committee has the effect of giving the authorities a *carte blanche* to detain leaders and close churches. In the last eighteen months, over 1,200 churches have had their crosses forcibly removed. Large red crosses once topped almost every church, in contrast to the government buildings with the gleaming red star. Churches are being built at breakneck speed, not always awaiting building permissions (which are frustratingly slow in coming). Using the new law, provincial officials are closing down on the new found freedoms, which since 1975, churches have enjoyed.

Repression leads to Growth

Curiously, and even gloriously, the government requirements enforced upon the church in 1949 have been the very factors which have led to its survival and growth. There are four main reasons for the accelerated growth. Firstly, the requirement that places a limit on the number of people that can gather for a meeting. This led to Christians meeting in small groups, often unregistered, which grew, split and multiplied. It is classic cell growth theory in enforced action. Secondly, the burning of Bibles and wrecking of church premises led to a scarcity of Bibles. The scriptures, because they were rare, were cherished, memorised and handed on. The scriptures were honoured and known in a new way. Thirdly, the family groups became crucial and the Christian faith was carefully handed on by respected elders in the family to following generations deliberately and systematically. This led to intentional faith sharing in the extended family relationships. Fourthly, not only the sense, but also the reality of being oppressed purified the Christian movement of nominal faith. Those that remained committed as Christians were deeply devoted to Christ and the Church. These four factors built the church silently in the community and the new found freedoms have enabled congregations to build churches and, in many provinces, to evangelise openly.

It is a humbling experience to meet church leaders in the cities and surrounding areas of Wenzhou, Shanghai and Nanjing. Almost everyone over thirty is one generation from starvation. Many were sent, certainly pastors, lawyers and graduates, for 're-education' and forced hard labour in the Cultural Revolution. The faces of older members betray the hard life they have endured. The huge development of industry in China over the last thirty years cannot hide the suffering many have undergone. Some of the churches visited would accommodate seating for 4,000+ and many are full each Sunday. The best assessment from the Pew Research Centre dates from 2010, the most recent year for which data is available, when they calculated that China had some fifty-eight million Protestants and about nine million Catholics in both official (Three Self Patriotic Movement) and unofficial churches. Some estimates are considerably higher and, because in the rural areas no-one is counting, frankly no-one knows. Much is made of the differences between the official and what used to be called the 'underground' church. The 'family' churches, as the Chinese Christians prefer to call them, are making links in many provinces with the official leaders. Indeed some 'family' churches are seeking registration with the government because that way they can request land to erect a church building.

Methodism in Hong Kong

The Methodists came early to Hong Kong. The British claimed Hong Kong for the Empire in 1841 and by 1844 there was a regular Class Meeting, of 'declared Wesleyans', in the home of Methodist layman, Rowland Rees, working with the Royal Engineers. Despite a request to the Conference of 1846 to send a minister to Hong Kong, the Revd Dr Jabez Bunting, a leading minister, declared such a venture impossible. However a farm labourer and Local Preacher from Pickering, George Piercy, felt the call to China and arrived in Hong Kong 'fresh from the plough' in 1851. Piercy came with 'a believing heart, a firm spirit ... not to be thwarted by absolute impossibilities'. In 1853 the Wesleyan Methodist

Missionary Society relented and sent two newly ordained students from Richmond College with a letter of ordination for Piercy. He was ordained as he read it! Hong Kong was the stepping off place for a new mission field in China.

The work in Hong Kong fluctuated according to the number of Wesleyans who came as soldiers and sailors. In 1893 the first garrison church was opened in Wan Chai on a plot of land leased for 999 years at one dollar per annum. It quickly became known as the 'English Methodist Church' for service personnel and government officials and their families. This was rebuilt in 1965 as the 'Methodist Church (English Speaking)' and is now being redeveloped as the 'Methodist International Church' into a twenty-two storey new Methodist Church and Hong Kong Conference Office.

Today, the Methodist Church in Hong Kong comprises of about 10,000 members in twenty-five local churches in four Circuits served by twenty-three Ordained Ministers, twelve Deacons and over one-hundred lay workers. The church has schools, nursery to secondary, five social service centres employing over 1,500 people, a retreat centre and separate retreat bungalow and a simple mountain lodge. Last September they organised a youth event for over 2,000 young people who are part of Methodist Churches. The church is young and alive with hope and faith.

What is it that we can now learn from this vigorous church?

1. **Spirit of Adventure** – for that is where faith takes you.

The entrepreneurial culture of Hong Kong affects the church. Members and committees are prepared to take a risk. Whilst being full of faith, they are also savvy and astute in their approach to decision making. Development and change are expected, welcomed and prayed over.

However, this spirit of adventure is not based on the prevailing culture or the visionary ability of the Hong Kong Methodists, but on a confidence in God. There is the active belief that there is a God and that the living, transforming God will be present in the worship of the church and the lives of Christians. Under these circumstances church life is a passion and not a duty. Despite living in a busy culture where people are time-poor, volunteers are really committed to working for God.

This confidence in God gives rise to hope and the expectation of growth; a desire for the deepening of faith; a commitment to reaching out to share faith with others and an urgency to serve those in need.

Prayer in the midst of this church culture becomes exciting. In March this year, MIC held a Church Stewards' meeting, leading to a Church Council discussion, out of which came excitement to seize hold of God in prayer. Members have formulated a prayer team across all our congregations, started a prayer garden each week for intercessory prayer and on the second Sunday of each month a Prayer Powerhouse of gathered, focussed, believing corporate prayer. In addition we are planning prayer walks and have started a prayer *WhatsApp* for intercessors which is used regularly to 'ping' prayer requests and items for rejoicing.

This spirit of adventure has been tested in the last year by the congregations of MIC who left the much loved but very inadequate building, in June 2014. Subsequently we have witnessed its destruction and the erection of a twenty-foot steel fence around the site. Presently the foundations are being dug. The construction will take until the end of 2017 before a renewed ministry will be possible through the redeveloped building. An adventure of faith tested in prayer and pocket!

2. Seizing opportunities – it's a kingdom thing.

Bamboo scaffolding is the illustration I offer to describe the attitude of the Hong Kong Methodist Church. It is remarkable thing to see a fifty storey building surrounded by bamboo scaffolding lashed together with plastic tape, reinforced half inch plastic tape, but tape simply tied nevertheless. Not an inch of steel, a clamp or bolt to be seen. Bamboo is preferred by construction firms here because it is flexible and moves in the typhoons, high winds, rains, heat and humidity which are experienced in Cantonese weather. Bamboo appears at first sight fragile but it is strong and flexible. Similarly the church here is nimble and flexible which adds to its strength.

It is a flexibility in which, if a congregation does not flourish in a part of Hong Kong, the church moves the congregation to another housing estate to test if it will bear more fruit in the new location. Often the British Methodist intuition, where a congregation struggles, is to throw resources at it, thus diverting energy, finances and ministry time to bolster a failing cause. There is in the bamboo culture a willingness to close, move and change.

The history of the Hong Kong Methodists forging opportunities is evidenced in the uniting of two strands of Methodism. When the Maoist revolution cast out missionaries in 1949 those who remained in the Far-East streamed into Hong Kong and Taiwan. Thus the British inspired *Wei Li Kong Hui* 'Follow the Way' church (the Cantonese parallel to the English Methodist Church), worked side by side with the United Methodist *Tsun To Kung Wooi* 'Defend the Truth' church, significantly enlarged post 1949. Forty years ago, in 1975, the two united and in 1987 the English Methodist Circuit transferred from the British Conference to become a circuit within the Hong Kong Conference. They now speak with one voice.

It is courageous vision which enables the church to seize opportunities. Reaching out from the first English Methodist Church came the building of the Cantonese Methodist Churches in Wan Chai (1937) and Kowloon (1950) with others at Yau Ma Tei. Now twenty-five local churches, many of which are in leased premises on a floor of a building, seek to worship and serve this community with energy and vision.

The present plans for the redeveloped MIC building take the maximum opportunity to build as high as possible. There will be a basement floor and twenty-two floors going up with nine floors for MIC plus Methodist Social Services, the Conference Office, four floors of accommodation and a Sky Chapel at the top. The church is also in negotiations for establishing a new work among Filipino workers in Macau.

3. Engaged in Community – for this is God's world.

From the beginning of the Methodist Church in Hong Kong, it has looked outwards to the needs of others. Very early Methodists established a home for sailors and soldiers who were passing through the port of Hong Kong. It was a caring ministry for service personnel far from home. The Ministers were also chaplains to the garrison. Indeed there is widespread respect for the church as a whole because of the long and honourable tradition of working with the poor.

The need for education saw the church establish schools and as thousands of Chinese came in 1949 and again in the 1960s, the church built 'villages' on the hillsides of Hong Kong to provide simple, safe housing for people who otherwise would live in shanty towns. The Methodist involvement meant the villages were called 'Epworth', 'Asbury' and 'Wesley'. When the Vietnamese boat people arrived in hundreds and were placed by the authorities in high fenced 'camps' on isolated islands surrounded by treacherous tidal waters, the churches visited and ran children's events. They were involved in a leper colony, and a mission supporting orphan children.

Today there are five social centres sponsored by the Methodist Church. They receive fifty percent of their funding from the government but the rest is underwritten and raised by the church. The numbers of social workers are measured in hundreds working with families, young people, counselling and support for the elderly, with budgets in millions of dollars. It is an enormous undertaking.

During autumn 2014, 'Occupy Central' exploded onto the roads of Hong Kong and the proximity of the Chinese Methodist Church in Wan Chai enabled the church to become a front line centre for medical aid and distribution of water, food and support for the young people involved. It was not uncontroversial, but the Minister and President, the Revd Tin Yau Yuen, and his colleagues determined this was a gospel work to be undertaken. The team from MIC were able to support this work. It should be said that the Methodist Church also offered support to police and members of their families, especially where in some cases the parent was in the police and the child was in the protest. The church leaders also engaged with politicians, urging moderation and dialogue. Moderation was in part achieved, especially at the end of the protest. Meaningful dialogue, however, was a casualty of the post-Occupy attempts at conversation.

4. Growing - in Christ.

The Methodist Church in Hong Kong, as well as the church in China, has only known growth, especially in the last seventy years. Not an easy growth, but a committed and determined process.

The Chinese cherish the Bible. The extraordinary truth is that the Amity Press in Nanjing produces ten-million

Bibles each year. Most are in Chinese script but also in many languages which are distributed around the world. That is, more bibles are printed in Nanjing, China than anywhere else in the world.

This is the Church of the Holy Word, Nanjing. Built to seat 5,000 - bigger than needed because "God is making more Christians". It is one of 238 churches in Nanjing.

To be standing in the vast print room of the Amity press is deeply impressive, both in the numbers of Bibles coming off the presses every two seconds, and the caring employment regime established by Amity. The Chinese, in towns and villages across the nation, receive the Bible eagerly and read it avidly. Similarly, the church in Hong Kong has extensive numbers of Bible study groups including *Disciple* in all its forms.

Growth requires a deepening of faith. Not just to know more, but to become deeper and more rounded Christians. The Methodist Church in Hong Kong is a relatively small church which has established and supports a retreat centre, intentionally seeking to create a culture for church groups to deepen their faith.

Lavish hospitality is a significant part of Asian culture which encourages growth and fellowship. In a village in rural Wenzhou, after visiting the church started by the Revd Ernest Cooper (a 'Joyful News' Evangelist who became a Methodist Minister), we were treated to a sumptuous tasty meal of chicken and rice all cooked in a single wok over a wood burning stove. Similarly the community at MIC has a vast capacity for hospitality. The deeply Wesleyan theme of 'All May Come' is significant, for God is a welcoming God.

A sign of growth is the generosity of the church. The view of some people, often in Britain, when looking at Hong Kong is that everyone is rich and therefore the church can afford all kinds of things (including its new building). It is true that people are generous with time and ability. It is not true that the congregations of the Methodist Church in Hong Kong are full of rich people. The difference is that church members tithe their income. Tithing is considered normal, not unusual, is preached about annually and that has a significant effect on what becomes possible. For instance, the Revd Tin Yau Yuen, who was President in 2012-2015 challenged the 10,000 Methodists to give, on top of normal giving, a pledge of $10,000HK in each of four consecutive years. That would bring the $400HK million that will be required to cover the redevelopment of MIC. The request for $10,000HK or £850 per year is certainly possible and many people are giving significantly beyond that.

5. Collaboration and Community – for we are one in Christ.

Being involved in an international church in Hong Kong makes one think seriously about community and what it means. International residents do not quite fit in the local community. So much is different in Hong Kong Chinese culture; it is at once attractive, compelling and intriguing, as well as hot and humid! Something extraordinary happens every day to assail the senses. So in this context, international people reach out to each other and to local professional Chinese. They look for unity and build consensus. The danger, of course, is that people look for like-minded people and live in an expat bubble. At its best, however, such international community encourages mutual sharing, which enables people to flourish in the multi-national setting, building on their own culture and embracing new opportunities and people.

In such a context, the role of story becomes so much more powerful - not to illustrate the truth, but to convey truth. We see it in the power of a spoken testimony of faith. The Chinese word *Guanxi* contains the idea – the ability to share my story as the reality of my world.

This is reinforced by the Chinese cultural understanding of 'face'. It is important not to be the cause of someone losing face in public. No-one has a verbal argument publicly. For even if you win the argument, you lose face because you caused another to lose face. So delicate matters in the life of the church are discussed at length in an attempt to find a compromise, a way in which all sides agree. Thus meetings can be long! However issues are resolved to a point at which we find harmony in the decision. There are few votes and never any losers.

What is really compelling about the Methodist Church here is that connexionalism has traction in the life of the church. The Asian value of harmony means that the discussions focus on the things that build up. It is not just a cultural notion, but has real effect in the discussion of delicate issues such as stationing. All twenty-five ministers of the twenty-seven churches are in the room at the annual and open discussion of stationing.

6. Holiness and Harmony – rediscovering our roots.

Being in the East and having opportunity to read in the library of Chung Chi Divinity School has helped me to find a new language to speak about holiness. It will require further study and writing (a project yet to be completed), but this much is clear. We know Wesley described holiness, or full salvation, as the 'grand depositum' with which God had graced the Methodist movement. This suggests that it is the main and overall theme which comprehensively includes the various aspects of Wesley's view of what was the main purpose of the fledgling Methodist Church. It was the theological and spiritual lens through which he viewed the mission and ministry of the work of the people called Methodists.

Sadly, it quickly became a romanticised notion and was marginalised in most Methodist theology, misunderstood in ecumenical circles and almost entirely rejected in British Methodism.

It is my contention that we need to search for a new language to convey the theological scope and practical implications of scriptural holiness. It is my judgement that the language of the east offers a new way of speaking about Wesleyan holiness. Asian spirituality describes the wellsprings of growth in holiness in terms such as enlightenment, flourishing, transcendence and harmony. Using these terms to describe Wesleyan holiness offers a refreshing new language for us to consider. For instance:

Searching to understand the very heart of God's purpose for us assumes there is openness to God's Word, willingness to respond to the prompting of the Holy Spirit, and commitment to follow in God's way: to follow the *Tao* (pronounced *Dao*), the Way of Jesus. Following means being transformed by God's grace in the whole of our being. God is the transcendent source of all things and through this triune God comes an inexhaustible spring out of which all life and movement flow. We will only find wisdom and harmony as we are exposed to God, and shaped by God's truth and love. Holiness brings enlightenment because it exposes us to a deepening awareness of the triune God and opens us to greater awareness of what God is doing in the world. Being closer to the holy being of God brings greater clarity to the issues of the secular world of politics, trade and financial dealings. Holiness propels us to engage prophetically and pastorally with the big issues of the day.

Such holiness will inevitably lead to harmony with the social order where people are fulfilling their obligations for the welfare of society. The outcome of holiness, being filled with the love of God, leads to human flourishing which has an impact among the community in which people live and work. A dynamic force of God's challenging and transforming love is released through people. Whilst such devotion is personal it has cosmic implications, for from the wellsprings of spirituality come the grace and justice of God which overflow for all people. This is God's radical way of being involved in the affairs of humanity. Such holiness has implications for our responsibilities to live in harmony with the created order, to be good stewards of the world's resources, to ensure that all have enough, that the poor and marginalised are cared for.

Such language releases us from the received wisdom of earlier holiness writing, that it is a personal spiritual experience, and assists us to see holiness as the significant description of all that God has raised Methodism to be and to do.

My contention is that we should seek to retrieve this Wesleyan holiness teaching from the shadows of church history and give people a vision of what might be, and what people might become. Engaging in such a task will require wisdom and creative thinking; exploring the language and images will lead to visible expressions of holiness and harmony. I commit myself to that journey.

How can we pray for Hong Kong and China?

Challenges, China and the future
No-one should doubt the determination of China and its President Xi Jinping to assert China's place in the Pacific and as an economic powerhouse in the world. China will not yield to foreign pressure and will not tolerate foreign

interference in its affairs. Christians are considered 'free thinkers' and therefore can be allied with subversive foreign interference which undermines the Communist Party. The National Security Law passed on the 1 July this year by the National People's Congress Standing Committee has the effect of giving the authorities a *carte blanche* to detain leaders and close churches. Pray for the church members and leaders in provinces such as Zhejiang and its major city of Wenzhou.

The 'umbrella revolution' of October 2014 was focussed on the issue of who can vote to choose the candidates for the Chief Executive of the Legislative Council. Beijing offered universal suffrage, but only for candidates favoured by Beijing. That was rejected. However the political dis-ease and social unrest has deeper causes. According to the South China Morning Post, Hong Kong faces a prolonged period of political stalemate and economic instability. There is long standing discontent with what people perceive to be unresponsive and unrepresentative government; chronic income stagnation; growing inequality; a soaring cost of living driven by ever rising housing prices, and depressing employment prospects for the young, especially those without university qualifications.

Pray for good governance in Hong Kong, and for the church leaders making representations about transparency, democracy and honesty.

Pray for the Methodist International Church, for wisdom and vision as the redeveloped building rises from the ground. The opportunities for this international church, which will have at least nine congregations, are immense. There are teams which are already planning and preparing for the work which will start as the church opens in 2017.

Pray for the Hong Kong Methodists, that they will have the energy and ability to match its vision for the work of the church in Hong Kong. Pray as the Hong Kong Conference appoint a new Superintendent for MIC to start in the summer of 2016. Pray for the ongoing and developing mission and ministry of MIC in Wan Chai and this region.

Thank you for this opportunity to share with you the wonders of this remarkable church and the inspiring place of Hong Kong. Grace and peace be with you.

Postscript:
To understand the Chinese authority's mind-set, one has to have a grasp of the troubled history of the last 150 years. It is against this perspective that they approach contemporary issues relating to foreign influence.

There is a received wisdom that the Chinese were ruthlessly punished by the Dutch, Portuguese and British in the nineteenth century and the Japanese in the twentieth century. Unscrupulous British traders began forcing Indian opium on Chinese consumers which led to the Opium Wars (1839-42 ending with the Treaty of Nanjing and again a further debilitating conflict 1856-60). When the Qing rulers tried to resist, the gunboat diplomacy of the British bullied China out of millions of silver dollars. The 'unequal treaties' of the nineteenth century brought the powerful Qing dynasty to its knees, leaving its people slavish addicts unable to resist the British who claimed Hong Kong and imposed trade agreements which favoured the British.

The wars of the twentieth century brought terrible deeds to the cities of China, the most horrific being the rape of Nanjing. The Japanese army captured Nanjing on 13 December 1937 leading to massacre, rape and looting. It is estimated that over 300,000 civilians and disarmed combatants died over a period of six weeks.

This 'century of humiliation', as it is called, at the hands of imperialism ended in 1949 with the triumph of Mao Zedong and communism. The story is recounted in school textbooks and influences present thinking about foreign policy. It leads to a culture of suspicion about foreign influence and thus China will not yield to foreign pressure and will not tolerate foreign interference in its affairs. The Tiananmen Square uprising was of 1989 was blamed by the Chinese authorities on 'Western bourgeois liberalism'.

It is, however, a curious thing that under the Presidency of Mao more than seventy million people died as a direct result of his policies (see the books by Jung Chang especially *MAO the Unknown Story*). The much vaunted agricultural policy revolution entitled the Great Step Forward was an absolute failure leading to the famine and the death of thirty million. None of this is published in China. Mao's portrait continues to hang above the Gate of Heavenly Peace and beams across Tiananmen Square. It is truly a nation of contradictions.

GHM

DISCUSSION QUESTIONS
to explore chapters one and two

Question One
(a) Have you ever heard a sermon which seemed to offer truth without grace? If so, what was the impact on you and why do you think you responded or reacted that way? What different reactions might have been felt by other members of the congregation?

(b) Have you ever heard a sermon which seemed to offer grace without truth, making it sound too easy to follow Christ? If so, what was the impact on you and why do you think you responded or reacted that way? What different reactions might have been felt by other members of the congregation?

Question Two
In the postmodern and post Christian world, the idea of absolute truth and an all-embracing meta-narrative has become unpopular. Are all truths in the Bible non-negotiable, or do some offer room for reinterpretation? If so how do we know the difference? Can we be certain what the Biblical writers meant? How do we find out? How dogmatic can we appropriately be about the requirements of Christian living in today's world? Does context make a difference or not?

Question Three
(a) If you were given some parts of the Sermon on the Mount for your preaching theme, and came to verses 31 and 32 about divorce, and you knew that several members of the congregation were divorced and

remarried, in what way, if any, would that affect your preaching? How can you preach the Biblical text faithfully with pastoral sensitivity?

(b) If you were preaching on Romans 1:18-32 and became aware that in your congregation there was a cohabiting gay couple, in what way, if any, would that affect your preaching?

(c) If you were preaching on one of the healing events in the ministry of Jesus, and knew that there would be a person in the congregation in a wheelchair, in what way, if any, would that affect your preaching?

(d) If you were planned to preach in a church which had recently had a significant fallout, with several people leaving as a result, how, if at all, would that affect the content and delivery of your sermon?

Question Four
a) What sort of things prevent you from hearing God speak when you are listening to a sermon?

b) In the light of the chapters you have read, why do you think it is important to preach both grace and truth?

c) Have you ever heard a sermon which, in its delivery, was lacking in grace? How did that show? What can we learn from this?

CONCLUSION
Paul Wilson
Development Worker,
Methodist Evangelicals Together

Margaret Parker and Chris Blake have ensured that we see grace and truth as inextricably linked. It is as we preach with grace and truth that the Holy Spirit brings the living word out of the written word. We must not forget that the perfect incarnate Son of God, who preached the truth, drew the largest crowds of sinners because he embodied grace. The advice given to a minister entering a new appointment was, 'Once the congregation know a minister loves them, they will receive the truth preached.' Similarly the Revd Graham Slater, past principal of Hartley Victoria College, noted in the critique of a student's sermon that while he heard the truth, there was a distinct lack of grace. Therefore, he advised that every sermon must be checked to ensure that both grace and truth are present.

Margaret and Chris have reiterated this in their thoughtful and insightful chapters and illustrations. At a time when different views of scripture on subjects facing the church are being considered and debated, it is essential that evangelical expository preaching has grace and truth present in equal measure. At an everyday level, their experience in ministry has reminded us of the variety of situations faced by members of a congregation. A particular passage may be a word of comfort for some, but a word of rebuke, correction or call to righteousness for others (2 Timothy 3:16). The preacher, whether in a pastoral relationship with a congregation or itinerant, must speak the truth in love (Ephesians 4:15).

In the Synoptic Gospels, Jesus' teaching is often introduced with, 'I tell you the truth ...'.[46] Professor Lindars comments that, in John's Gospel, this is present with a double emphasis, 'Very truly I tell you' (NIV, 2011).[47] He adds this 'use has no real parallel ... and seems to have been a special feature of Jesus' authoritative style of speaking.'[48] As noted by Margaret, these encounters between Jesus and others may present a challenge, given in love to the individual or group. To Nicodemus, it is the ultimate challenge to be 'born again' (John 3). No wonder people thought Jesus taught as one who had authority (Mark 1:27), but with compassion for those with whom he spoke (John 6:34). As preachers of the gospel, truth and grace must go hand in hand to offer God to those in our congregations.

In his book, 'Preacher, keep yourself from idols', Derek Tidball warns about the misuse of authority in preaching. The following may be signs of such abuse:

- Preaching 'at' people we disagree with;
- Being dogmatic in areas of dispute;
- Going beyond what the scripture says;
- Not distinguishing between what is primary and secondary;
- Preaching the programme or latest fad rather than the text;
- Beating up our congregations rather than encouraging them;

---

[46] For example Mark 3:28, 8:12, 9:1 & 41 plus 9 other references and parallels in Matthew and Luke.
[47] For example John 1:51, 3:3,5,11 plus 25 other references.
[48] Lindars, B. (1987) *Gospel of John*. Grand Rapids, MI: Eerdmans, p120.

- Preaching beyond the text to preach political, social or economic policy; or,
- Voice personal prejudices on everything.[49]

The authority of the preacher is to allow the Holy Spirit to lead us into all truth and fill us with the love of God for our congregations.

Billy Graham's style in preaching was, 'The Bible says'. The Bible was his authority. However, he is widely quoted as saying, 'It is God's job to judge, the Holy Spirit's job to convict and my job to love'. In this great evangelical preacher, we see the evidence of grace and truth. Perhaps this is why God used him to bring so many to faith.

In Howard Mellor's chapter on the growth of the church in Hong Kong and China, we see grace and truth at work. Despite opposition, full of the grace of God, the early missionaries preached the gospel. Taking the clothing of the Chinese, they embodied the gospel in all they said and did. During the persecution, the Chinese treasured scraps of the Bible. One generation passed the truth of scripture to the next. The challenge for the church in the West is to have the same thirst for scripture and to share the gospel with our families. Preachers have a significant role in this. We are to share our joy of scripture, by our tone, enthusiasm, body language and example as well as by our words. It may be that another Margaret will be challenged not only to offer Bible reading notes but be

---

[49] Tidball, D. (2011) *Preacher, Keep Yourself from Idols*. Leicester: Inter-Varsity Press, p. 44-47.

encouraged to read the Bible and begin a life of discipleship.

We await with interest Howard's reflections on the challenge of the East to a new understanding of scriptural holiness. However, as preachers we must begin to see our calling to spread scriptural holiness. By preaching the sum of the Word of God, we will enable congregations to see how they can be kingdom builders wherever they are.

In, *Every Good Endeavour,*[50] Tim Keller expounds the teaching of Genesis about work. The book seeks to encourage the reader to see how their work can bring God's influence into all areas of life. It is an example of opening the scriptures to speak into people's lives. The challenge for the preacher is the application. Keller points out that his preaching showed people that they have kingdom influence not only by witnessing but doing their work well. He does not limit the ministry of work simply to teachers and carers, but to creatives and carpenters, shop cashiers and financiers, government and raising children. That cutting edge in our preaching releases the congregation to develop scriptural holiness in their lives and spread scriptural holiness in their spheres of influence.

The church in China is growing, and Howard encourages us to be challenged by the principles of growth. There is one challenge facing every preacher. China has gone through, and is going through, a period of persecution. Tertullian said, 'The blood of the martyrs is the seed of

---

[50] Keller, T. J. (2014) *Every Good Endeavour: Connecting Your Work to God's Plan for the World*. London: Hodder & Stoughton.

the church'. The challenge to preach grace and truth may indeed cause the preacher to suffer. There will be those who, at the door, by letter or via the Superintendent Minister confront us about our evangelical preaching. It may not be 'spoken in love'. It may be one comment amongst many, good comments, but we all know as preachers which comments we remember.

In preaching the sum of scripture, we are seeking to reveal the grace of God who, despite our rebellion, calls us home to a restored, renewed relationship with him. This meta-narrative of Scripture focusses on the cross, where we see the truth of our sinfulness and the superabundance of God's grace. In response, we are called to take up our cross and follow Jesus (Matthew 10:38). Paul calls us to be living sacrifices (Romans 12:1). Preachers are called to preach the gospel when we feel like it and when we do not, in churches who will receive it and in those who may oppose it (2 Timothy 4:2). Such preaching is costly. However, the evidence of history in China, Hong Kong and every circuit and church in the United Kingdom is that such faithfulness bears much fruit.

> In the presence of God and of Christ Jesus, who will judge the living and the dead, and in view of his appearing and his kingdom, I give you this charge: preach the word; be prepared in season and out of season; correct, rebuke and encourage – with great patience and careful instruction (2 Timothy 4:1-2).